# *DEADLY* MOSQUITOES

By Abigail Richter

Gareth Stevens
Publishing

Please visit our website, www.garethstevens.com. For a free color catalog of all our high-quality books, call toll free 1-800-542-2595 or fax 1-877-542-2596.

**Library of Congress Cataloging-in-Publication Data**

Richter, Abigail, 1971-
Deadly mosquitoes / Abigail Richter.
    p. cm. — (Small but deadly)
Includes index.
ISBN 978-1-4339-5740-6 (pbk.)
ISBN 978-1-4339-5741-3 (6-pack)
ISBN 978-1-4339-5738-3 (library binding)
1. Mosquitoes as carriers of disease—Juvenile literature. 2. Mosquitoes—Juvenile literature. I. Title.
RA640.R53 2011
614.4'323—dc22

2011006081

First Edition

Published in 2012 by
**Gareth Stevens Publishing**
111 East 14th Street, Suite 349
New York, NY 10003

Copyright © 2012 Gareth Stevens Publishing

Designer: Michael J. Flynn
Editor: Greg Roza

Photo credits: Cover, (cover, back cover, pp. 2-4, 7-8, 11-12, 15-16, 19-24 background texture), pp. 1, 5, 6 (larva, pupa), 14, 17, 20 Shutterstock.com; p. 6 (eggs) Paul Zahl/National Geographic/Getty Images; p. 6 (adult) Getty Images; p. 9 iStockphoto.com; p. 10 Tyler Stableford/Aurora/Getty Images; p. 13 Gazimal/Iconica/Getty Images; p. 18 Justin Sullivan/Getty Images.

Printed in the United States of America

CPSIA compliance information: Batch #CS11GS: For further information contact Gareth Stevens, New York, New York at 1-800-542-2595.

# CONTENTS

Words in the glossary appear in **bold** type the first time they are used in the text.

# SHOO, FLY!

A mosquito is a small fly. It has a skinny body, six long legs, and two long wings. When a mosquito flies close to your ear, you can hear it buzzing. The sound is made by its quickly moving wings.

Mosquitoes bite to get blood! The location of the bite becomes swollen and itchy. To make things worse, several mosquitoes often bite at the same time. Mosquitoes are known as real pests, but they can also be deadly.

## DEADLY DATA

There are more than 3,000 kinds of mosquitoes in the world. About 200 are found in the United States.

Mosquitoes live everywhere except Antarctica and central Greenland.

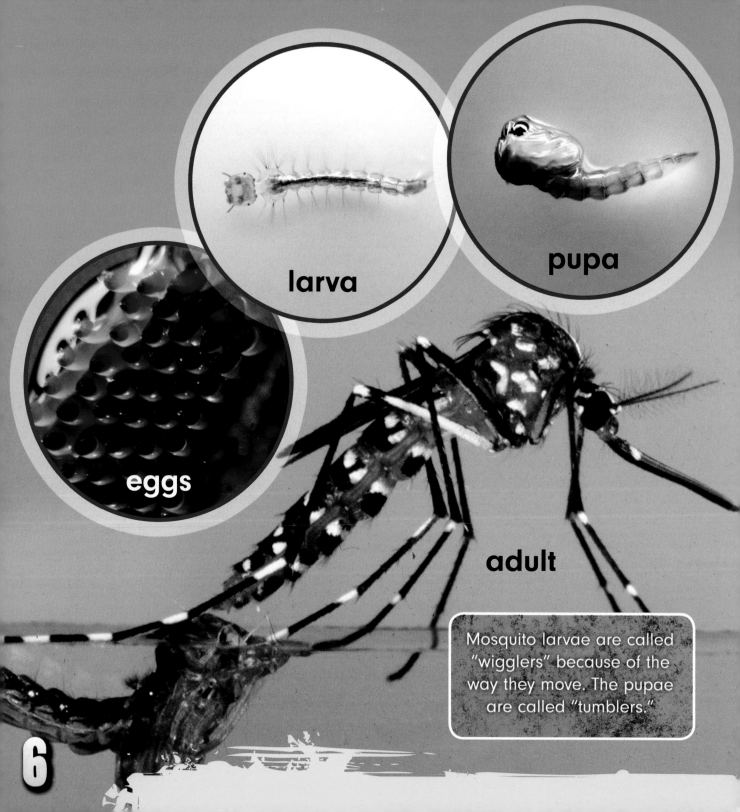

larva

pupa

eggs

adult

Mosquito larvae are called "wigglers" because of the way they move. The pupae are called "tumblers."

# MOSQUITOES GROWING UP

Female mosquitoes lay eggs in or near water. After 2 or 3 days, mosquito **larvae** break out of the eggs. The larvae look like tiny white worms. They live at the water's surface and breathe air. They can dive underwater to avoid trouble.

In about 5 or 6 days, the larvae form a hard case around themselves. Now they're called **pupae**. Pupae don't eat, but they can move around. Adult mosquitoes break out of the cases in about 3 days.

## DEADLY DATA

The singular form of "larvae" is "larva."
The singular form of "pupae" is "pupa."

# ADULT MOSQUITOES

Adult mosquitoes don't eat blood. They eat **nectar**. Male and female mosquitoes **mate** within 3 to 5 days after breaking out of their pupae cases. Males live for about a week.

After mating, female mosquitoes go in search of blood. They need it to help their eggs grow. Females have special mouthparts that allow them to break skin and suck up blood. Then they lay their eggs. Females may live long enough to lay up to 3 batches of eggs.

## DEADLY DATA

Female mosquitoes can sense body heat and the **chemicals** in our breath. This makes it easy to find human blood!

Mosquitoes lay "rafts" of eggs on the surface of standing water, or water that isn't moving.

9

This hiker is being bitten by many mosquitoes. A large group of mosquitoes is called a swarm.

# WHAT A PEST!

Mosquito bites can ruin picnics and cookouts. However, they can cause more serious problems as well. Sometimes mosquitoes bite farm animals and make them sick. This can cause the animals to lose weight. Cows may make less milk, too.

Mosquitoes are more than just pests. They can be deadly! Mosquitoes can carry **parasites** and **viruses** that cause illnesses. Female mosquitoes spread illnesses when they bite a sick animal and then bite a healthy animal.

## DEADLY DATA

Scientists have discovered that one out of ten people is more likely to be bitten by mosquitoes because of the chemicals in their body.

# MALARIA

Malaria is caused by parasites called **protists** that live in blood. It's spread by a kind of mosquito that lives in hot locations. When a mosquito bites someone with malaria, it takes some of the parasites with it. The mosquito spreads the illness when it bites another person.

Malaria symptoms, or signs, include chills, headaches, coughing, and tiredness. Malaria can also cause worse problems such as trouble breathing, blackouts, and liver failure. Without treatment, malaria can lead to death.

## DEADLY DATA

There have been no reported cases of malaria in the United States since the early 1950s, even though the mosquito that spreads it lives here.

Wearing a net like the one shown here is a good way to avoid mosquito bites.

This is an Aedes mosquito.
It's the kind that spreads
yellow fever.

# YELLOW FEVER

Yellow fever is caused by a virus that lives in blood. It's spread by a type of mosquito that lives mainly in hot areas of Africa and South America. Once in someone's blood, the virus grows and spreads throughout the body.

Among other symptoms, the yellow fever virus harms organs in the body, such as the liver and kidneys. The harm to the liver can make a person's eyes and skin look yellow. Yellow fever can lead to blood loss and death.

## DEADLY DATA

Illnesses carried by mosquitoes are known as mosquito-borne illnesses. "Borne" means "carried by."

# DENGUE FEVER

Dengue (DEHNG-gay) fever is caused by four viruses spread by mosquitoes. It's common in hot areas all over the world, including southern Florida.

The main symptoms of dengue fever include fever, rash, and headache. It can also result in backaches, swollen body parts, low heart rate, low body temperature, and sweating. Very few cases of dengue fever cause death. However, children under 10 are at risk of more deadly symptoms. These include stomach pain, blood loss, and a swollen heart.

## DEADLY DATA

Dengue fever spreads faster than any other virus carried by mosquitoes.

This man is spreading a fog that contains chemicals that kill mosquitoes.

17

Mosquitoes can grow in the standing water of unused swimming pools, posing a serious health risk.

# WEST NILE VIRUS

West Nile virus is spread by mosquitoes that get the virus from birds. It's found mainly in Africa and parts of Asia, but has spread around the world. The first cases of West Nile virus in the United States occurred in 1999.

Mild symptoms of West Nile virus include fever, headache, rash, and body aches. Other symptoms include sleepiness, a stiff neck, uncontrollable shaking, and blackouts. The greatest danger is swelling of the brain, which can lead to death.

## DEADLY DATA

West Nile virus is one of several similar illnesses spread by mosquitoes. All of them can lead to swelling of the brain.

# STAYING SAFE

Countries all over the world are trying to stop the spread of mosquito-borne illnesses. It's important to rid areas of standing water, which is where mosquito larvae grow. Standing water can include puddles and unused swimming pools. Some sprays keep mosquitoes from biting. These sprays are called "repellents" because they chase away, or repel, bugs. Other ways to stay safe include using mosquito netting over beds, fixing broken screens and windows, and having an area sprayed with a **pesticide**.

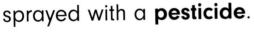

# FACTS ABOUT MOSQUITO-BORNE ILLNESSES

| | malaria | yellow fever | dengue fever | West Nile virus |
|---|---|---|---|---|
| **cases in 2010** | 350–500 million | about 200,000 | 50–100 million | 981 (in the United States) |
| **deaths in 2010** | about 1 million | about 30,000 | about 22,000 | 45 (in the United States) |
| **parasite or virus** | parasite | virus | virus | virus |
| **symptoms** | chills, headaches, coughing, tiredness, trouble breathing, blackouts, liver failure | fever, chills, tiredness, weakness, aches, throwing up, bleeding, kidney and liver failure | tiredness, fever, rash, low heart rate, low body temperature; in some cases, bleeding, swollen heart | fever, headaches, rash, sleepiness, stiff neck, uncontrollable shaking, blackouts, swelling of the brain |

# GLOSSARY

**chemical:** matter that can be mixed with other matter to cause changes

**larvae:** bugs in an early life stage that have a wormlike form

**mate:** when a male and a female come together to make babies

**nectar:** a sweet liquid made by flowering plants

**parasite:** a living thing that lives in, on, or with another living thing. The parasite gets benefits but harms the other living thing.

**pesticide:** a chemical used to kill pests, such as mosquitoes

**protist:** any one of a large group of living things that are mostly so small they can only be seen with a microscope

**pupae:** bugs that are changing from larvae to adults, usually inside a case or cocoon

**virus:** a very tiny thing that can cause illness when it enters the body

# FOR MORE INFORMATION

## BOOKS

DiConsiglio, John. *Blood Suckers! Deadly Mosquito Bites.* New York, NY: Franklin Watts, 2008.

Kalman, Bobbie. *The Life Cycle of a Mosquito.* New York, NY: Crabtree, 2004.

## WEBSITES

**Hey! A Mosquito Bit Me!**
*kidshealth.org/kid/ill_injure/bugs/mosquito.html*
Read more about mosquitoes and how to avoid getting bitten.

**Mosquitoes**
*www.historyforkids.org/scienceforkids/biology/animals/arthropods/ mosquitoes.htm*
Learn more about mosquitoes and see a video of one sucking blood!

# INDEX